Special to God.

Luu
Jandu
M.

I
AM
PRETTY
ENOUGH

30 DAYS OF ENHANCING YOUR SELF-IMAGE, SELF-ESTEEM, SELF-WORTH AND SELF-CONFIDENCE

This book will help enhance self-image, self- esteem, self-worth and self-confidence in girls who may struggle in these areas.

What is self-image? "The idea one has of one's abilities, appearance, and personality".

What is self-esteem? "The confidence in one's own worth or abilities; self-respect."

What is self-worth? It could be used as "another term of self-esteem."

What is self-confidence? "A feeling of trust in one's abilities, qualities, and judgment."

These definitions were provided by Google's search.

Special note: If you need to, please use the dictionary to help you understand the meaning of certain words used throughout this book.

I

AM

PRETTY

ENOUGH

30 DAYS OF ENHANCING YOUR SELF-IMAGE, SELF-ESTEEM, SELF-WORTH AND SELF-CONFIDENCE

CONTENTS

INTRODUCTION...7

DAY 1: TELL YOUSRELF THAT YOU ARE BEAUTIFUL...9

DAY 2: EMBRACE YOUR BEAUTY 11

DAY 3: BE HAPPY WITH THE WAY YOU LOOK...............13

DAY 4: YOUR SMILE IS BEAUTIFUL.....................................15

DAY 5: YOU LOOK LIKE A BEAUTIFUL FLOWER............17

DAY 6: LOVE THE SKIN YOU ARE IN 19

DAY 7: BE KIND TO YOURSELF...21

DAY 8: SAY SOMETHING POSITIVE ABOUT
YOURSELF..23

DAY 9: SHOW YOURSELF APPRECIATION FOR
SOMETHING GOOD YOU DID..25

DAY 10: BE AND DO YOUR BEST...27

DAY 11: BELIEVE IN YOURSELF...29

DAY 12: BE GENUINE..31

DAY 13: DO NOT EVER COMPARE YOURSELF TO
SOMEONE ELSE 33

DAY 14: DO NOT EVER REJECT YOURSELF 35

DAY 15: LIFT YOUR HEAD..37

DAY 16: RESPECT YOURSELF 39

DAY 17: TAKE CARE OF
YOURSELF 41

DAY 18: DO NOT SETTLE FOR LESS 43

DAY 19: TURN NENGATIVE IMAGES INTO POSITIVE
IMAGES 45

DAY 20: TURN NEGATIVE THOUGHTS INTO POSITIVE
THOUGHTS 47

DAY 21: SURROUND YOURSELF WITH POSITIVE
MINDED PEOPLE 49

DAY 22: ENCOURAGE
YOURSELF 51

DAY 23: ENCOURAGE SOMEONE ELSE 53

DAY 24: DO NOT BEAT YOURSELF UP OVER A MISTAKE
YOU MADE 55

DAY 25: MAKE A GOOD DECISION 57

DAY 26: LET GO OF THE FEAR 59

DAY 27: HAVE COURAGE TO DO SOMETHING
NEW 61

DAY 28: YOU CAN 63

DAY 29: YOU ARE GREAT 65

DAY 30: YOU WERE CREATED FOR A PURPOSE 67

INTRODUCTION

One of the most important things a girl could ever do is love every part of herself, from the top of her head to the soles of her feet. But this is not easy for every girl to do. It is hard for some girls to love every part of themselves due to having poor self-image, self-esteem, self-worth and self-confidence. When a girl struggles in these areas, it can have a negative effect on her. She can easily find herself going through life being fearful, making bad choices, settling for less, having unhealthy friendships and relationships, and so many other unfavorable things.

I struggled with poor self-image, self-esteem…as a child and a young adult. I later learned that these things were preventing me from moving forward. After I developed a personal relationship with God, I realized that He was the One who was responsible for creating me, and He did not make any mistakes on me.

7

I began to thank and appreciate my Creator for my uniqueness ("one of a kind, one of me") and beauty. I learned to love myself the way God loves me. I started telling myself: "I am a beautiful Gem and God loves me." These words served as my self-esteem booster. They helped me to form a different outlook on life and become more confident about my future.

If you feel that you are not as pretty as you would like to be and you struggle in the areas that have been mentioned, then I want to encourage you to get ready to embrace the new you. This book is for you. You are going to start feeling good about yourself, and by the time you finish reading this book, you will learn to love every part of you. You too will be able to look in the mirror and confidently say, "I am a beautiful Gem and God loves me."

DAY 1

TELL YOURSELF THAT YOU ARE BEAUTIFUL

Your voice has power and it needs to be the first one heard when it comes to saying things that will make you feel good about yourself, so I encourage you to say "I am beautiful" as often as you can, and you will begin to see it and feel it.

You may have family members, friends, and others who may tell you that you are beautiful, and there may be some people who feel that you are not, and they may even tell you. But you do not have to ever accept any negative comments that are intended to make you feel bad about yourself.

Psalm 139:14 "I will praise You, for I am fearfully and wonderfully made."

Look in the mirror and say this: "I am a beautiful Gem and God loves me."

Prayer: God, I pray that You help me to see myself as You see me. Do not let me be afraid to tell myself that I am beautiful, even when others say that I am not. Amen.

DAY 2

EMBRACE YOUR BEAUTY

You have to embrace every part of you, from the top of your head to the bottom of your feet. You must learn to celebrate your inner as well as your outer beauty. If you cannot embrace your beauty, then you cannot really expect anyone else to do it. So, go ahead and wrap your arms around the beautiful you and continue to cherish all of you.

Psalm 139:14 "I will praise You, for I am fearfully and wonderfully made."

Look in the mirror and say this: "I am a beautiful Gem and God loves me."

Prayer: God, I pray that You help me to embrace every part of me today and every day of my life going forward. Amen.

11

DAY 3

BE HAPPY WITH THE WAY YOU LOOK

Girl, you look amazing. You must learn to simply be happy with the way you look. God made every single thing perfect about you. He did not make any mistakes on you when you were being formed, and that should make you happy. Your hair is the right texture and length. Your ears are formed just right. Your nose is perfectly shaped. Your eyes have a sparkle and they make you shine. Your lips are the right size.

The rest of your body is beautiful just the way God made it. Nothing has to be removed or altered. Everything can be left the way God made it. All you have to do is just be happy with all of you.

Psalm 139:14 "I will praise You, for I am fearfully and wonderfully made."

Look in the mirror and say this: "I am a beautiful Gem and God loves me."

Prayer: God, I pray that You help me to be happy with my looks and be thankful that you formed me just the way you wanted me to be. Amen.

DAY 4

YOUR SMILE IS BEAUTIFUL

When you smile it can make you have a great feeling on the inside as well as on the outside. Your smile also shows a part of your beauty, it makes you glow and it creates an inviting look. Do you know that people want to be around you when they see a smile on your face? Your smile can help brighten their day. It sends a message to others that you are happy, grateful, and joyful. It can also send a message that you are confident and that you are not going to let anything or anyone steal your smile. When you frown it sends an opposite message to others. So, I encourage you to smile more from this day forward.

Psalm 139:14 "I will praise You, for I am fearfully and wonderfully made."

Look in the mirror and say this: "I am a beautiful Gem and God loves me."

Prayer: God, I pray that You help me to realize that I have a reason to smile and that I only need to focus on those good and positive things that will make me smile more every day. Amen.

DAY 5

YOU ARE LIKE A BEAUTIFUL FLOWER

I would like for you to think about a red, yellow, pink, purple, white, blue, orange, green...flower for a brief moment. As you get a picture of that flower in your mind, can you really see how beautiful it is? If one of the colors mentioned are your favorite, then you might think it is even more beautiful, right? Well, I want you to know that you are beautiful just like a flower.

You not only blossom in the spring or summer time, you blossom every single day, at home, at school, in your community, etc.

Psalm 139:14 "I will praise You, for I am fearfully and wonderfully made."

Look in the mirror and say this: "I am a beautiful Gem and God loves me."

17

Prayer: God, I pray that You bless me to blossom every day just like a flower. Amen.

DAY 6

LOVE THE SKIN YOU ARE IN

As you look around, you will find that there are many who have the same color of skin as you, and some have a different color of skin. But you were created by the same God just as others.

He created you to be who you are and love who you are in your smooth black, white…skin. Regardless of your race, the shade of your skin, you are special to Him and He loves you unconditionally. And He wants you to "love the skin you are in."

Psalm 139:14 "I will praise You, for I am fearfully and wonderfully made."

Look in the mirror and say this: "I am a beautiful Gem and God loves me."

Prayer: God, I pray that You teach me how to love the "skin I am in." Amen.

DAY 7

BE KIND TO YOURSELF

You can be kind to yourself by doing something you really enjoy—reading a book, spending time with your friends, shopping, etc. You can be kind by striving to excel academically every time you grace the halls at school. You can be kind by saying good and positive things about yourself.

You can be kind by loving who you are. You can be kind by respecting yourself. You can be kind by forgiving yourself when you say or do something to hurt or disappoint others. There are so many other ways you can be kind to yourself. So, I say to you, start being kind to yourself today.

Psalm 139:14 "I will praise You, for I am fearfully and wonderfully made."

Look in the mirror and say this: "I am a beautiful Gem and God loves me."

Prayer: God, I pray that You teach me how to start being kind to myself now, and let it continue as I grow each day. Amen.

DAY 8

SAY SOMETHING POSITIVE ABOUT YOURSELF

I encourage you to say at least one positive thing about yourself. Before you say it, let me share that even as a child you have many great, personal qualities that you may or may not be aware of. For example, you may be talented, smart, fun, inspiring, friendly, etc.

You may go ahead and say something positive about yourself now. I want you say it with confidence. Okay, now you should feel good about what you just said about yourself.

I want to let you know that you should never only rely on other people to say good things about you because you may not hear it often from others.

You must say good things about yourself; therefore, if other people do not ever say it, you will still feel good about yourself and all of your great attributes ("a quality or feature").

Psalm 139:14 "I will praise You, for I am fearfully and wonderfully made."

Look in the mirror and say this: "I am a beautiful Gem and God loves me."

Prayer: God, I pray that You bless me to always be able to say something good about myself, even if I do not ever hear other people say it to me. Amen.

DAY 9

SHOW YOURSELF APPRECIATION FOR SOMETHING GOOD YOU DID

Clap your hands and pat yourself on the back for every single good thing that you have done. If you did a chore at home without your parents having to tell you to do it, then clap your hands…if you made the honor roll, then you should clap your hands… if you completed a task before the deadline, then you should clap your hands again…if you did something special for a family member, a classmate, a teacher, a friend, or a church member, then you should clap your hands for what you did. You should show yourself appreciation because you deserve it.

Psalm 139:14 "I will praise You, for I am fearfully and wonderfully made."

Look in the mirror and say this: "I am a beautiful Gem and God loves me."

Prayer: God, I pray that You bless me to celebrate the good things I accomplish. Help me to always be humble and give You praise and thanks for all the good things I have done and the good things I will continue to do as I grow. Amen.

DAY 10

BE AND DO YOUR BEST

I want you to know that God created you to be and do your best while you are here on earth. There is a special strength and ability you have that will help you to succeed in life as you grow. You must always work hard and rely on your inner strength and ability to produce the best results. Most importantly, you must rely on God because He is the One who created you and knows what is best for you.

Never ever settle for less. Never ever do the bare minimal. For example, if you have to take a test on a particular day at school, make sure you invest the time in studying for it so that you can make a high mark on it. You must always…do your best in all that you embark on in life. If you are ever slacking in an area, then you must take note of it and strive to become better and better each day.

Psalm 139:14 "I will praise You, for I am fearfully and wonderfully made."

Look in the mirror and say this: "I am a beautiful Gem and God loves me."

Prayer: God, I pray that You help me to always work hard and strive to be and do my best in every endeavor in life. Amen.

DAY 11

BELIEVE IN YOURSELF

I encourage you to believe in yourself. Once you set your mind on doing a particular thing, you should not stop until you complete it. If you hear someone say that you cannot do it; that means you should work harder to prove them wrong.

As you grow, you will cross paths with people who are not going to believe in you, and they will say negative things about you. You cannot allow what people say about you stop you from moving forward.

You must believe in yourself, even when people talk about you, when you make a mistake, and when things seem not to be working out for you. You have to be your greatest believer. And one thing to always remember is that God believes in you and your abilities because He is the One who gave them to you. He knows that you can do anything with Him by your side.

Psalm 139:14 "I will praise You, for I am fearfully and wonderfully made."

Look in the mirror and say this: "I am a beautiful Gem and God loves me."

Prayer: God, I pray that You help me to believe in myself. Do not let me doubt or second guest myself. Help me to understand that I can do anything with You by my side. Amen.

DAY 12

BE GENUINE

You have to be genuine with yourself and with others. God did not make anything fake about you; therefore, He does not intend for you to hide behind a mask or pretend as you journey through life. You are a real person who is not perfect—no one is perfect. You may have a weakness that you are dealing with now. You may lack a quality that you desire to have. And that is perfectly okay. It is okay for you to even communicate your imperfections or faults with others.

When you are real it is allows you to be transparent ("easily to be seen through; clear") about what bothers you, hurts you, confuses you, etc. As you grow, make sure to always be genuine, honest and pure.

Psalm 139:14 "I will praise You, for I am fearfully and wonderfully made."

31

Look in the mirror and say this: "I am a beautiful Gem and God loves me."

Prayer: God, I pray that You help me to be genuine and have pure motives. Amen.

DAY 13

DO NOT EVER COMPARE YOURSELF TO SOMEONE ELSE

One thing for certain that you should never do is compare yourself to someone else or try to become someone else. You are uniquely different, and so is everyone else. It is perfectly okay to admire a person's looks as well as their talents and their strengths, but if you try to become them, you will only disappoint yourself.

Today, you can have confidence in knowing that God has already equipped you with everything you need to succeed in life. You have qualities that another person may not have, and they have qualities that you may not have. If you lack a quality that someone else has, it does not mean that you are not worthy or unimportant, nor does it mean that you cannot do a specific task—you can do anything you set your mind to

33

do. In order to prevent comparing yourself to someone else, you must focus solely on whatever you aspire to do, and do your very best to excel in it.

Psalm 139:14 "I will praise You, for I am fearfully and wonderfully made."
Look in the mirror and say this: "I am a beautiful Gem and God loves me."

Prayer: God, I pray that help me not to compare myself to other people. Amen.

DAY 14

DO NOT EVER REJECT YOURSELF

It is easy to have a thought of rejecting yourself when you are rejected by others. If someone has ever made you feel like you are not worthy or deserving of something, you may have thought that you were actually not good enough for whatever it was; therefore, you rejected yourself, maybe not even realizing that is what you were doing.

I want you to know that you have no reason to reject yourself because you are the "Apple of God's eye." That means you are important and valuable to Him. Let me share that God will never reject you, and He does not intend for you to do that to yourself.

Psalm 139:14 "I will praise You, for I am fearfully and wonderfully made."

35

Look in the mirror and say this: "I am a beautiful Gem and God loves me."

Prayer: God, I pray that You never let me reject myself. Amen.

DAY 15

LIFT YOUR HEAD

It is not uncommon to hold your head down if you do not feel good about yourself, if you feel that you are unattractive, and if people make jokes and talk about you on a regular basis.

You may tell people that you are okay if they were to ask why you are holding your head down when you are really hurting deep within. I know how that feels. I was a person who used to hold my head down a lot because I had low self-esteem. I pretended I was okay when I was sad, confused and hurt by what people said about me and how I felt about myself.

As time progressed, I felt better and better about myself, and I began to lift up my head. I want to encourage you to lift your head, stand tall and walk like the beautiful person you are from this day forward. I did it and you can do it, too.

Psalm 139:14 "I will praise You, for I am fearfully and wonderfully made."

Look in the mirror and say this: "I am a beautiful Gem and God loves me."

Prayer: God, I pray that You help me to lift my head, even when I am feeling low at times. Amen.

DAY 16

RESPECT YOURSELF

You must always have the utmost respect for yourself, and then you will find that it will be easier for others to respect you. There are so many ways to respect yourself. I want to share a few with you. Make sure you dress appropriately; do not wear clothes that are too tight and revealing. You should have wholesome, calm, polite conversations with others; you do not have to feel the need to communicate in a disrespectful and rude manner. Always keep a positive attitude. It is also important to keep your character intact (complete). When you do these things, then you are showing others that you respect yourself.

Psalm 139:14 "I will praise You, for I am fearfully and wonderfully made."

Look in the mirror and say this: "I am a beautiful Gem and God loves me."

Prayer: God, I pray that You to help me to always respect myself. Amen.

DAY 17

TAKE CARE OF YOURSELF

You can easily neglect yourself by failing to take care of yourself. It is that simple. I encourage you make it a habit to start taking care of yourself now while you are young. You can start getting your proper rest so that you can think clearly. You can start eating healthy and exercise a few times a week. You can start making sure you are clean and have healthy hygiene daily. You can make sure your hair is nice and neat before you leave home. If you notice that something is not right with your clothes, hair, etc. before you leave home to go to school or somewhere else, then you should let your mother or guardian know so that they can help you. When you take good care of yourself, you will look and feel good about yourself.

Psalm 139:14 "I will praise You, for I am fearfully and wonderfully made."

Look in the mirror and say this: "I am a beautiful Gem and God loves me."

Prayer: God, I pray that You help me to start taking care of myself so that I can always feel good when I go places, even when I am at home. Amen.

DAY 18

DO NOT SETTLE FOR LESS

I want to encourage you to never settle for less. Let me help you understand in a quite simple way what it means to settle for less. If you settle for less, then that means you feel that you only deserve the bare minimal and you are okay with accepting whatever it may be, despite your desire for something greater.

Allow me to use a similar example that I used before. Let's just say that you are preparing to take a test at school, and you desire to make an A on the test, and you know that it is going to take hard work, dedication and a commitment to study in order to make an A, but you tell yourself, "I will be fine with making a C." In this case, you will be settling for less. On the other hand, if you make up your mind that you are going to make an A, and you do what is needed to earn that grade, then you will not be settling for less. You will be very proud of yourself for getting what you actually deserve.

As you grow, I want you to remember to never ever settle for less in any aspect of your life; that includes in your relationships, friendships, when you start your career, etc. You deserve only the best, so expect the best. And again, do your best.

Psalm 139:14 "I will praise You, for I am fearfully and wonderfully made."

Look in the mirror and say this: "I am a beautiful Gem and God loves me."

Prayer: God, I pray that You help me to never settle for less. Amen.

DAY 19

TURN NEGATIVE IMAGES ABOUT YOURSELF INTO POSITIVE IMAGES

Have you ever taken a picture of yourself on your cell phone that you did not like or has someone else taken a picture of you on their phone or camera that you did not like? You probably said, "I don't like that picture, it's ugly." Well, the truth is you may not have liked it. But one thing you must realize is that, regardless of what you were wearing, how your hair was styled, the way you smiled, etc. while taking the photo, the person on the picture is still you. It is a person you have to learn to accept.

I want you to know that if you have a poor self-image of yourself, then you are going to grow into an adult thinking of yourself in a negative light. You are going to think that you are not good enough or pretty enough to do certain things in life.

In order to change your outlook, you must start visualizing yourself in a positive light. Again, start telling yourself you are beautiful. Start thinking you are beautiful, even on a day you do not feel like it. You can even draw beautiful pictures of yourself. The positive words you speak concerning your image can and will allow you to start seeing yourself as the beautiful person God intends for you to see in "the skin you are in," every time you look in the mirror.

Psalm 139:14 "I will praise You, for I am fearfully and wonderfully made."

Look in the mirror and say this: "I am a beautiful Gem and God loves me."

Prayer: God, I pray that You help me to see myself the way you intend for me to from this day forward. Amen.

DAY 20

TURN NEGATIVE THOUGHTS ABOUT YOURSELF INTO POSITIVE THOUGHTS

It is the negative thoughts that produce the negative images. If you continue to have negative thoughts about yourself, then you will continue seeing yourself in a negative light. You will think of the worst. You will easily attract and surround yourself with negative people. You will even act in a negative manner.

But once you start to turn those negative thoughts you have about yourself into positive thoughts, then you will not only see yourself in a positive light. You will have a clearer view all the potential you have, and you will have more confidence to do things you never thought you could do. You will even expect better results in life. You will find it easier to attach yourself to people who will be a positive influence in your life.

Psalm 139:14 "I will praise You, for I am fearfully and wonderfully made."

Look in the mirror and say this: "I am a beautiful Gem and God loves me."

Prayer: God, I pray that You help me to think positive every day. Amen.

DAY 21

SURROUND YOURSELF WITH POSITIVE MINDED PEOPLE

I want you to know that when you surround yourself with positive-minded people, you can look forward to being motivated, inspired and supported. These are the kinds of people that will help you to become your best self. They will tell you good things that will build you up and not tear you down. They will let you know that you can do a particular task because they are the ones who believe in you.

You will learn as time progresses that people who are positive-minded are often those who are seeking to make a difference. They are people who do not want to waste any of their precious time on negativity. They too want to be around those who think and act like them.

Psalm 139:14 "I will praise You, for I am fearfully and wonderfully made."

Look in the mirror and say this: "I am a beautiful Gem and God loves me."

Prayer: God, I pray that You lead and guide me and surround me with positive-minded people. Amen.

DAY 22

ENCOURAGE YOURSELF

What a great feeling it is to encourage yourself sometimes! There will be times in life when you will have to encourage yourself because people will not always be there to encourage or push you when you need it. Allow me to share this example to help you understand what I mean by this. Example: You may have a project at school that has been assigned to you, and it has to be completed by a certain date. You may feel like giving up or not doing it because the project does not seem easy to do and will take a lot of time to complete. You may not even have a clear understanding of what to really do, even after your teacher explains it, but you still have to do it because it is required to pass the class. Even though you may feel like giving up, this is a time you

51

will have to work hard, encourage and push yourself until it is done.

I provided this example to help you understand that you will need to learn how to encourage and push yourself because as you grow there will be some things in life that you will have to do that are not going to be so easy, and you are not always going to have people around to help you.

You may be faced with something today that requires you to encourage yourself. I want to let you know that it is not that hard. You can do it. Keep the confidence and remember to always believe in yourself.

Psalm 139:14 "I will praise You, for I am fearfully and wonderfully made."

Look in the mirror and say this: "I am a beautiful Gem and God loves me."

Prayer: God, I pray that You help me to start encouraging and pushing myself, especially when I need it the most. Amen.

DAY 23

ENCOURAGE SOMEONE ELSE

What an even greater feeling it is to encourage someone else! Your parents, siblings, friends, and even your teachers need to know that they can count of you to encourage them today. You can do that by simply telling them they are important and they can do it, and you are there to help them. You may think, "How can I help someone and I am just a child?"

I want you to know that anyone can offer words of encouragement to someone else. A person is never too young or too old to say something good to someone; that is what encouragement is. Just as you may feel sad sometimes or feel that you cannot do a specific thing, other people can feel this way too, and they need to hear some positive words.

Psalm 139:14 "I will praise You, for I am fearfully and wonderfully made."

Look in the mirror and say this: "I am a beautiful Gem and God loves me."

Prayer: God, I pray that You help me to say something encouraging to someone from this day forward. Amen.

DAY 24

DO NOT BEAT YOURSELF UP OVER A MISTAKE YOU MADE

We as human beings are going to make mistakes in life. A lot of mistakes we tend to make are because we may not have the knowledge of something. Quick example (a similar one used before): Say you make a mistake on a test in class. You made notes and studied for the test, but there was an unfamiliar question on the test when you took it, so you ended up choosing the wrong answer. You went back to look at your notes and found out that you actually did not have any notes for that question. So you really did not know the answer; that is why you made the mistake.

I want to encourage you to never beat yourself up over a mistake you make or have made. However, you must learn and grow from your mistakes, not repeat them. If you

55

ever find yourself repeating a mistake, then that means you have not learned from it. On the other hand, if you make a mistake and not repeat it, then that means you have learned a valuable lesson and grown from it. It feels good to not repeat a mistake. Let me also share that you can learn from other people's mistakes, too.

Psalm 139:14 "I will praise You, for I am fearfully and wonderfully made."

Look in the mirror and say this: "I am a beautiful Gem and God loves me."

Prayer: God, I pray that You help me to not repeat any mistakes that I may make as I grow. Allow me to learn and grow from my mistakes. Amen.

DAY 25

MAKE A GOOD DECISION

You are going to have to make decisions throughout your life. You are going to make bad decisions, and you are going to make good decisions. Either decision you make, it will result in a consequence ("a result of an action").

I want to encourage you to start making good decisions while you are a child. In order to do this, you will need to think before you make a decision. Also, you need to always pray to God about a decision before you make it. If you do this, and really listen to His instructions, you will find yourself making good decisions every single time, and you will feel good about the outcome. This will build your confidence even more.

Psalm 139:14 "I will praise You, for I am fearfully and wonderfully made."

Look in the mirror and say this: "I am a beautiful Gem and God loves me."

Prayer: God, I pray that You help me to always make the right decision throughout my life. Amen.

DAY 26

LET GO OF THE FEAR

You can easily find yourself at a "stand still" if you are a fearful person. Having fear prevents you from moving forward in life. It stands in the way of great opportunities. Fear makes you think of the worst. You can actually miss a blessing that God has for you if you have fear.

As you grow, it is my hope and prayer that you become successful, and I believe you will. However, I must let you know that you will need to let go of any fear because it will hinder you as you strive to become successful.

Psalm 139:14 "I will praise You, for I am fearfully and wonderfully made."

Look in the mirror and say this: "I am a beautiful Gem and God loves me."

Prayer: God, I pray that You to help me to let go of the fear. Amen.

DAY 27

HAVE COURAGE TO DO SOMETHING NEW

There may be something new you want to do, but you are afraid to do it because it may seem hard to do or you do not feel like you are good enough to do it. You must have the courage to "do it anyway." You will feel so much better, knowing that you have at least given it a try. Never give up.

Psalm 139:14 "I will praise You, for I am fearfully and wonderfully made."

Look in the mirror and say this: "I am a beautiful Gem and God loves me."

Prayer: God, I pray that You give me the courage to do something new. Amen.

DAY 28

YOU CAN

You may have heard someone say, "Girl, You cannot sing. You cannot dance. You cannot cheer. You cannot be a majorette. You cannot play volleyball. You cannot run; you too slow. You cannot be the class president. You cannot make the honor roll." You may have heard them say a number of other things that you could not do or be. I am certain you thought about what someone said that you could not do…and then you felt that you could not do it.

I want you to know that when people say that you cannot do something, they really do not believe in you. In some cases, they could be jealous of you because it is really them who cannot do it.

If you feel that you cannot do something, mainly because someone told you that you could not, allow me to speak life into the

core of your spirit and tell you that you can. Yes, you can do some things you never imagine doing. Keep believing in yourself and be the best in whatever you are doing.
Psalm 139:14 "I will praise You, for I am fearfully and wonderfully made."

Look in the mirror and say this: "I am a beautiful Gem and God loves me."

Prayer: God, I pray that You help me to have the confidence to do anything I aspire to do, and help me to know that I can do it with You by my side. Amen.

DAY 29

YOU ARE GREAT

I want to let you know that you were great before you ever knew you existed. Before you ever cried your first tear as a baby, you were great. Before you were ever disappointed by your parents, siblings, friends, or someone else, you were great. Before you were ever talked about by anyone, you were great. Before you ever made a mistake, you were great.

You are still great today and you will continue to be great. You will be great in the position of the model, nurse, doctor, lawyer, teacher, author, singer, counselor, dentist or whatever you want to be when you become an adult.

From this day forward, I want you to expect great things to happen for you every day. I also encourage you to start telling yourself that you are great.

Psalm 139:14 "I will praise You, for I am fearfully and wonderfully made."

Look in the mirror and say this: "I am a beautiful Gem and God loves me."

Prayer: God, I pray that as I grow You let me be reminded of my greatness and help me to be great in all that I do throughout my life. Amen.

DAY 30

YOU WERE CREATED FOR A PURPOSE

You were created for a purpose, just as every human being who exists in the world. As you grow you will understand more about what your purpose is in life. God created you because you are needed and important. What a wonderful feeling it must be to know that you are needed and important! You do not just exist—you exist for a reason far greater than you can even imagine and understand as a child. There is something specifically God wants you to do, and He has already given you the tenacity ("quality of being able to do something") to do it. Again, as you grow, you will have a clearer understanding of that specific thing that will cause you to make a positive, huge impact in the world.

There may be something you really find joy and fulfillment doing even now, while you are a child, and that may just be a small part of your purpose. Perhaps, you may like to sing, write, dance, help people, etc. Could you think of at least one thing you really like to do? Do you feel that you are really good at doing it? If you answered yes, then I want you to know that it may very well be what God has purposed you to do. Again, you will learn more about your purpose as you grow.

I encourage you to start praying to God, asking Him what your purpose is, and He will show you. He may show you in a dream or He may have your spiritual leader to share it with you or it may be revealed through your parents or some other way. Either way, just know that you were created for a purpose.

Psalm 139:14 "I will praise You, for I am fearfully and wonderfully made."

Look in the mirror and say this: "I am a beautiful Gem and God loves me."

Prayer: God, I thank You for creating me for a purpose. I pray that You make my purpose known until me in Your perfect timing. Amen.

~PERSONAL NOTES~

_____

_____

_____

_____

_____

_____

_____

_____

_____

_____

_____

_____

_____

_____

_____

_____

_____

~PERSONAL NOTES~

_____

_____

_____

_____

_____

_____

_____

_____

_____

_____

_____

_____

_____

_____

_____

_____

_____

~PERSONAL NOTES~

_____

_____

_____

_____

_____

_____

_____

_____

_____

_____

_____

_____

_____

_____

_____

_____

_____

~PERSONAL NOTES~

_____

_____

_____

_____

_____

_____

_____

_____

_____

_____

_____

_____

_____

_____

_____

_____

~PERSONAL NOTES~

_____

_____

_____

_____

_____

_____

_____

_____

_____

_____

_____

_____

_____

_____

_____

_____

_____

~PERSONAL NOTES~

_____

_____

_____

_____

_____

_____

_____

_____

_____

_____

_____

_____

_____

_____

_____

_____

~PERSONAL NOTES~

_____

_____

_____

_____

_____

_____

_____

_____

_____

_____

_____

_____

_____

_____

_____

_____

~PERSONAL NOTES~

_____

_____

_____

_____

_____

_____

_____

_____

_____

_____

_____

_____

_____

_____

_____

_____

_____

~PERSONAL NOTES~

_____

_____

_____

_____

_____

_____

_____

_____

_____

_____

_____

_____

_____

_____

_____

~PERSONAL NOTES~

_____

_____

_____

_____

_____

_____

_____

_____

_____

_____

_____

_____

_____

_____

_____

_____

_____

_____

~PERSONAL NOTES~

_____

_____

_____

_____

_____

_____

_____

_____

_____

_____

_____

_____

_____

_____

_____

CPSIA information can be obtained
at www.ICGtesting.com
Printed in the USA
FFOW04n2115111115
18394FF

One of the most important things a girl could ever do is love every part of herself, from the top of her head to the soles of her feet. But this is not easy for every girl to do. It is hard for some girls to love every part of themselves due to having poor self-image, self-esteem, self-worth and self-confidence. When a girl struggles in these areas, it can have a negative effect on her. She can easily find herself going through life being fearful, making bad choices, settling for less, having unhealthy friendships and relationships, and so many other unfavorable things.

In this book, the author is determined to make a positive impact on the lives of girls who struggle with poor self-image, self-esteem, self-worth, and self-confidence. She feels that if she can reach and teach them while they are girls, they will grow into healthy young women who will be in expectation of the best that life has to offer them. She desires for every girl to love every part of herself, have a healthy self-image . . . and become her best self. She believes that every girl who picks up this book and reads it, her life will be different and successful.

YOLANDA MARSHALL-NICKERSON, author, motivational speaker and evangelist. Yolanda has a passion to inspire and encourage everyone she crosses paths with. She speaks from a heart of compassion and has been used to make a difference in the lives of many. She believes that her commitment to serving God is by serving others. She has spoken at women's conferences, network meetings/luncheons, revivals, girls' detention centers, non profit organizations, senior citizens and retirement centers, etc. She is the founder of V2V Gems in the Making, a motivational, inspirational, self-empowerment, life-transforming initiative that is geared toward hurting and broken girls and women.

$8.00

ISBN 978-0-9833221-7-7

50800 >

9 780983 322177

Glimpse of Glory
CHRISTIAN BOOK PUBLISHING